PROUD MEMBER

[clmp]

COMMUNITY OF LITERARY MAGAZINES & PRESSES
W W W . C L M P . O R G

PUBLISHER: WWW.WFLF.ORG

Spontaneous

Poems by Victoria Dym

Chapbook Challenge Series Winner 2021

© 2021 Victoria Dym

Funding for this title provided by
the West Florida Literary Federation, Publisher

ISBN: 9798424773037

Editor: Katherine Nelson-Born

Cover Art: Christopher Anselmo Priore,
         Friends Embracing in a Snowy Landscape

Author Photo: Kelly Paxton

Cover Design: Sydney Zalewski

Table of Contents

for Cath

"Spontaneity is a meticulously prepared art"
~ Oscar Wilde

Alone With Moths

never had them in Pittsburgh
unlike Barbara
  her closets peppered with balls
  of Naphthalene, the toxic
  smell of storage

—closet moths—

in Florida, my walk-in
where I shelter from hurricanes
  is also home to their eggs
  larvae, cocoons, and the adults
  with their dusted crystalline wings

—closet moths—

I name them as they fly by
dart in and out of folded sweaters
and hangered shirts. I name them
  as they crawl up the wall
  worm larvae, bridled paper reins
  like racehorses to the ceiling

—closet moths—

And they're off: Misty Pines takes
the lead, Whispering Worm
    a close second, Closet Santa
    just a hair behind Rambino

—closet moths—

Turning down the homestretch,
Here they come: Mushroom Burrito
Little Edna, Uncle Thunder, Tall Tattoo
    Old Mook, Voodoo Dating
    tiny-size pests, turn to pets
    jockey the odds for a photo finish

How to Look Cool on the Internet

after Kaci Beeler

1. Post every hour on the hour to Facebook, Tik-Tok, Instagram, Snapchat, Twitter, Linked-In and YouTube

2. Score your posts with Rap Songs or Hip Hop

3. Point at things

4. Filter your face

5. Already be popular

6. Something something Minecraft

7. Have a dog that's a good boy

8. Or a cat with a weird face

9. Follow everyone, like everything, accept every friend request

10. Pay a consultant to get followers

11. Photograph your every meal, your take-out, your dine-in ones too

12. Get a lunch date with Mark Zuckerberg

Truth

after Natasha Trethewey

Everywhere you go will be somewhere
you've never been

Your pirate's soul, hoists the Jolly Roger
full of rum and gunpowder
and you sail the sea of highways
shore to asphalt shore

Even if it's the same place
it will be a different time

The talking exotic bird on your shoulder
is your conscience,
the cannonball in your gut is the tick-tick
ticking timebomb, a race to find buried
treasure, to find X that marks the spot

Truth is you'll never reach the horizon

Telephone of the Wind

muffled by moss, in Priest Point Park, Pacific Northwest

a rotary dial phone is affixed to a plywood rectangle

which is anchored to a century's old cedar.

next to the phone, a laminated marker:

Telephone of the Wind

connected to nothing but the wind,

its long attached spiraled cord, long enough

to reach the couple's two living children

who, united in sorrow with rain in their throats,

and knots in their hearts, are able to bond, make

the longest of long-distance calls to their lost,

beloved, eternally four-year-old, Joelle Rose.

1955

We're gonna rock around the clock tonight…

Rosa Parks refuses to move to the back of the bus, refuses to give her seat to a white passenger.

When the clock strikes two and three and four…

Disneyland opens in Anaheim, California, one-hundred-sixty acres of orange groves gone.

We're gonna rock rock rock 'till the broad daylight…

Swanson TV dinners, Coca-Cola in cans, Kellogg's Special K, McDonald's hamburgers, 15¢ and fries 10¢.

Five, six, seven o' clock, eight o'clock rock…

Polio vaccines in arms, In God We Trust
The $64,000 Question, I've Got a Secret

I Love Lucy,
Search for Tomorrow.

…rock rock rock…

Notes on Notes

When listening to music, I take notes,

close eyes, oscillate, day to night, then back

    breathe in, harmony, breathe out—theta, beta, gamma waves

    walk the forest, bathe in lavender, sunlight, beach, rocking chair

        flute = bird

        oboe is the duck

        cat, the clarinet

I sit, and when my blood whispers, I leave my body,

the genius of the ear

    seven thousand pages in one note, remove the rust

    in my joints, my brain

        grandfather = bassoon

        Peter is the violin, the viola, the cello

        wolf, the French horns

The headmaster of my elementary days, crowns me tone deaf;

I take note. Instead, sing my words on paper, to the dog, the pillow.

    I love the drums.

        gunshots = timpani, bass drum

Maxwell Calls

It's my birthday—Maxwell, my brother's son, my only nephew, calls.
He doesn't call very often.

Once, when he was about to ask his now wife to be his fiancé,
he called. That was a long one. He wanted my blessing.
He wanted his courage bolstered for the ask. She said yes.

Then, two weeks before the wedding, which had been postponed
due to the pandemic, rescheduled twice, Maxwell calls to ask if I
would write a poem, and speak it in front of his one-hundred guests.
I said yes.

He called after, while on his honeymoon, to thank me for the poem,
which I had framed for them, he told me that I had hit it *out of the park.*
We used to go to Pirates games and I was always there for Little
League.

He calls me Aunt Wacky, introduces me as such to his Marine buddies,
Paris Island graduation. We make each other laugh, share the same
sense-of-humor-DNA. It's my birthday, and Maxwell calls.

He's happy after a round of golf, a good score—his day off, so we talk
about his upcoming reenlistment dilemma, his father's, my brother's,
not-so-funny jokes, a recent training about Top-Secret Chinese missiles

that can jam our drones. *Maybe, we can all meet up in Las Vegas, soon?*
They have a machine gun shooting range in Vegas, his voice swells
with Little League excitement. *It's the best, Aunt Wacky, you'll love it!*
He likes guns and golf, and giggles when I ask him if he owns any guns
of his own. He says yes. A Glock and a shotgun. He wants to get a
rifle, explains the difference between the two.

                (I gave him green plastic Army men once
for 'his' birthday, remember him, on the floor, sounding out gunfire).

When Lady Liberty Steps Down from Her Pedestal

She shakes her statuesque pose, sheds her patina, walks alive
boards the ferry from Ellis Island to the Big Apple, finally,
after staring at its shimmering glow for centuries.

First thing, she exchanges her toga-robes for a pair of jeans, exchanges
her flat sandals for a mid-heel, buys her first bra, a push-up.

She uses the torch as a night light/ reading lamp—the Declaration
of Independence on her nightstand, one-room studio, murphy bed.

The first few nights, she falls asleep still wearing her crown, later
stowing it on the top shelf of the closet, along with the broken chains
that had adorned her feet, a secret nod to the end of slavery.

Day by day, she misses the adoration of *the tired, the poor, the huddled
masses*, instead, becomes them.

Her arm, sore from holding the torch for so long, begins to throb
when she learns that the vote for the first female president had failed
in 2016, learns that it was so close, learns about who had defeated her.

She writes in her journal: *All men are created equal.* Then scratches
out the word "men".

Beautiful and Dangerous

after Yusef Komunyakaa's "Slam, Dunk and Hook"

Cleats on feet, fresh cut field,
we girls play by different rules,
city campus, private girls' school.
We cradle our crosses, baby the ball
metaphysical practice for the future,
checking sticks clap-clash. We run
we run, we run, we shoot, we score.
Attack positions: first home, second
home, third home; it's all about home.
Starting now, we make our home
on this field, shin pads stuffed
navy-blue knee socks, black-watch
plaid pleated skirts, short navy shorts
underneath, navy blue uniform sweater;
we sweat, we sweat, we sweat,
tie the sweaters around our waists
crisp white tees with thistle insignias,
Fall crisp air that makes our thighs
and cheeks blush. We all want to win
the most important thing, long hair
in ponytails, whistled umps stop
the play, the Center is down, ball

to her head. We huddle around

to see blood drip from her nose,

both beautiful, and dangerous.

Snide & Snippy

for Martha

I make snide remarks and she makes snippy retorts.
We are superheroes in our sixties, show-women,
soul sisters, silent shell snatchers, high-school chums—

Boom Shacka-Lacka, Boom Shacka-Lacka

Sometimes, we snap and sway,
sing stories into prayers. Sometimes
we stretch, stargaze, shift *sick and tired*
into *tired and sick,* sculpt each other, sleep—

Boom Shacka-Lacka

I am snide & She is snippy.

Randomnes
s

When the sun made our hair turn golden, we were happy together

in Chicago, at Elsa's wedding, dancing haloes, lighting the night in

celebration.

Home remedies for itchy hard swollen bug bite: oatmeal, crushed ice,

honey, aloe vera,

baking soda, basil, vinegar, onion, thyme, lemon balm, witch hazel,

chamomile tea, garlic.

I'm afraid of men with chiseled abs, like I'm afraid of statues

                                    falling on me in museums.

Charred chick breasts stuffed w/ spinach & feta

        in oven 1 hr. & 45 mins, fall asleep

            no fire, unlike the chickpea incident

                        NYC

The upstairs neighbor screams out in her squeaky siren rage,

You're an asshole!

                    I imagine that she is looking into a mirror.

14

Spontaneous

Like the recoil when a wasp flies near

Quick-sudden-abrupt

Like instant coffee, instant oatmeal

Instant mashed potatoes

Instant chemistry—poof

Love at first sight, blink of an eye

Pavlovian-knee-jerk-reaction

A burst of applause, a burst

Spontaneous burst of applause

Spontaneous Human Combustion

Torso reduces to ash

Only part of the left leg remains

Mid-calf, shoe on

Out of Nowhere

In Bliss, Idaho at the Miracle Hot Springs, I dangle feet, submerge
whole body. *The Best Water on Earth, a sensational alkaline pH of 9.6.*
Soft to the touch, a kitten pool. I soak, mineral-water-happy.
Perrier bath. I am here to relax, here to heal old bones,
here for a miracle in these warm springs.

Ever since I caught the bouquet at Corry's wedding, I fantasize
about a spontaneous connection, the perfect storybook romance,
love as hot as these springs—hot. And then, he walks in, hangs
his blue robe on the peg to the right of my pink one, dangles feet,
submerges his whole body next to mine.

It starts to snow.

The Land of Snow and Woe

Suburban ranch homes all in a row
lights glimmer and glow; it's Christmas
I grow here as a child
in the land of snow and woe

I grow slow with dogs and birds
Neon Tetras darting to and fro
Jeff, my bro, a snake and a turtle
snow and woe, this is what I know

This, I know, I live blow by blow
hang mistletoe, as mother passes out
her rage, I tiptoe around; try to love
the snow, try to love the woe

Try to love her, but it's hard to show
love, no, just woe, in the land of snow

Back in the Day

Gullifty's restaurant in Squirrel Hill, Murray Avenue, cross between
a diner, a family eatery and a weekend jazz club, famous for its desserts
baked fresh daily:

Peanut Butter Truffle Pie

Killer Kookie

5th Dimension Cake

Chocolate Intemperance

They twirl around in two refrigerated lighted cases, next to the hostess
stand, making the wait for a table mouthwatering.

Back in the day, the hostess would ask, *Smoking?* —because
back in the day, there were smoking and non-smoking sections,
before the complete ban on cigarettes in restaurants.

And so, we stand there, by the swirling-twirling refrigerated, lighted
cases, back in the day, and the hostess asks her question and we pause,
my mother, a smoker, my fiancé, a vegetarian, a runner, a health-food
foodie and me, allergic to smoke, I say, *No smoking, please.*

We had picked my mother up at her Bloomfield apartment, (she had
abandoned the family home in Fox Chapel years after my father died)

18

and drove her to Gullifty's for lunch (she had no car of her own,
just DUIs). Larry wants to get to know my mother better
before the wedding.

We order orange juice, coffee for her, small-talk-weather, browse the
menu, and she is silent, steaming like her coffee, the corners of her
mouth turn down; she gets up suddenly, *I can't do this; I'm going home.*
She storms out, I call the waitress, tell her there's been an emergency.
I pay for the drinks, leave her a big tip. Larry gets the car.

We spot her walking and smoking on Murray Avenue, heading towards
Forbes. She ignores us, as Larry honks and tries to talk to her, across
the street, from the car window. She is stoic, a walking, smoking statue.
We double back, catch her on the right side of the street, convince her
that the two-mile walk is too much for her, and because it starts to spit
rain, and she has finished her cigarette, she huffs a sigh,
gets into the car.

Silent the whole way to her place, she slams the car door upon exiting.

Looking at the Face I Will Inherit—My Mother's Face

She exhales:

    long stream of gray smoke,

    smoke, that speaks the words she never spoke

She finds joy:

    still can blow a smoke ring when asked

    like she did as a teen, then grizzle-laughs, then phlegmy coughs

She's a master of:

    Civil War trivia, Gettysburg, Bull Run, Fort Sumter

    a history buff, a soldier for the southern troops, uniform of gray

She withers:

    end of days, ashen face, her face, my face, I memorize that

    weekend before her cloudy-gray Pittsburgh day turns black

Once

She told me once, if she told me twice, that I was a mistake, because

of a hole in the dried, cracked diaphragm, that sat in the faded blue box

shoved to the back of her nightstand drawer.

She told me that I was fat,

told me that *I* forced *her* to beat me,

to slap me,

to throw me

through the wall, down the stairs,

whip me with the belt,

the hairbrush, her stiletto heel, told me I should be happy for the roof

over my head, for the food on the table, the clothes on my back,

told me that I was stupid, that I needed

to *straighten up*, told me

that I was not-funny.

And she told me that my brother was conceived only to keep me

company. However, she would tell him, that she loved him,

after *his* beatings,

but never did I hear, *I love you* from my mother,

not once, not even as she drew her

very last breath.

Waterbordeauxing

Waterboarding	Waterbordeauxing
a form of torture	a form of self-torture
water is poured	alcohol is poured
intermittently, repetitively	intermittently, repetitively
sometimes a gag reflex	sometimes a gag reflex
can cause extreme pain	can cause extreme pain
brain damage	brain damage
and death	and death

-over and over, drink after drink, pour after pour

-slow torture

-hip flask

-instead of coffee in the cup

-the highest proof

-the feeling of drowning

-the surrender to abuse

22

What Happens After I Eat an Angus Beef Cheeseburger (Without the Bun) For the First Time in Nearly Two Years After My Doctors Tell Me to Eliminate Red Meat from My Diet Because of My Heart Condition And My High Cholesterol

Nothing.

Cornucopia

Daughter asleep in her own bed— me awake in mine (the night
before, we snuggle on the couch, faux-fur covers, giggle).
She—home from college, me—the empty nester no longer
(at least for this thankful week). Two cats asleep, with me, still in bed—
the last languish, the extra deep breath, arms overhead stretch
before the Macy's Day Parade, the 2010 National Dog Show—
intermittent cooking that starts with pumpkin pie, all the way
through to the salad with home-baked garlic croutons.
As I rise, I am thankful for plumbing, the troops that defend,
for that hallway lamp, for Harry Potter in Imax— grateful for the rain
that taps on the kitchen pane, in rhythm, as I crack two eggs.

Driving Home from Fernandina Beach

seat heat on— November AM
sun through the driver's window radiates
face and upper torso—46° outside
car clock, turn back time—turn into Racetrack,
park near the umbrellaed tables in the front—
shiny Cowbirds and Laughing Gulls
squibble-squabble about the drop in temperature,
vociferous about the possibility of errant trash-food.
I step out of my car's warm womb, walk through
the crisp windless day, cold air-shower on my skin
through my clothes, bathroom stop and breakfast.
My nose suggests hot dogs and corn husk tamales
on the stainless-steel roller grill, but my mouth
aches for Carl's Ice Cream, butter pecan on a cake cone.
Last night's salmon niçoise salad with yellow gazpacho
dressing, side of parmesan truffle-oil fries, is erased
with one lick. Inside the car, still hot, I swirl my tongue,
coat it with the confection, crunch the cone, crush
the tip in the paper holder, accidently-on-purpose
sprinkle the crumbs near the trash can. They squabble.

At the pump, the rich, dangerous smell of gasoline
somehow comforts me, fuels me to get back
on the road, drives me home from Fernandina.

Writing A Poem

Writing a poem is

    retelling a vivid dream to Barbara. The one where Diane

    is driving my car (I'm in the passenger seat), off the road,

    into the grass, through the woods, over a cliff, into a

    swimming pool that's marked by her tombstone. Before

    impact, I open the window and then swim out; Diane follows.

    She couldn't go through with her suicide

    and I am left with no car.

Writing a poem is

    watching the Muscovy from the water-streaked window

    sit still

    on the hill, in the rain,

    focus on their duck-bill faces.

Writing a poem is

    feeling the rain in my arthritic hand, a branding iron inside,

    2 PM, as dark as 9.

    I surrender to a nap, spritz a spray of Karma perfume,

    that my daughter bought me,

    birthday present, lemongrass, Brazilian orange,

    patchouli, spritz a spray

    on the zebra print velour couch throw, wrap it like a pastry crust,

    crimp it softly at my neck.

Writing a poem is

    loading the dishwasher, noting the difference

    between mechanical rain

    and the real thing,

    turning the baked potato for a second five minutes,

    anticipating its subsequent sour cream bath,

    slicing the Honeycrisp apple, coring it,

    imagining if the knife slips,

    counting the seeds.

    There are 6.

The Crow and the Poet

after CAConrad's reading

Like the twelve days of Christmas, only in the Spring,
the crow, black like a beautiful death,

brings the first gift, places it on the open windowsill,
the left bay windowsill,

shakes and taps the bent twig, once, twice, thrice,
before laying the treasure down.

The poet, in turn, places the twig, on the altar
and leaves a peanut on the sill, in gratitude.

That night, the poet dreams, of the crow bringing
gold nugget to the window.

The next day, the peanut is gone; in its place is
a round white nub of plastic.

Peanuts exchange for seed pods and berries, once, twice, thrice,
left, on the left bay windowsill.

Seeds from the Linden tree, varied leaf specimens,
yellow, red and green, a sliver of pine bark from the forest.

The poet imagines the crow's daily travels, selecting perfect gifts for
the poet, who arranges the crow's offerings on the altar

next to carnelian, amethyst, and rose quartz crystals. The poet sets out
water in a mini black ceramic ritual bowl, left bay windowsill.

The bird lingers longer, dunking peanut, dining-in, rather than take-
away. On the eleventh day, the crow brings a red, half-moon shaped

piece of cat food. The poet is vegan and they discuss this. On the
eleventh night, the poet dreams of a lover by the name of Earth,

bodies and minds entwine, sweat and salt. The dream turns to
nightmare when those in black robes and head coverings

rape and torture Earth. They scorch Earth, douse Earth in gasoline,
set Earth on fire.

On the twelfth day, the crow brings
a shiny, perfectly round piece of gold foil.

Whispers to the Wind

I wish that for one night
a man who I am dating
would make me dinner
at home
cooking while I read,
take a bubble bath, or nap
or write—
make a dessert that rivals
the ones I remember
from Gullifty's
back in the day.
****

I live alone, have
since 2010—
dated for a handful
of months, and always
ate out.

I hope I can find that
someone special
to cook with, everyday,
handsome like Bourdain
sweet imaginative banter
like Cake Boss Buddy

travel, food adventure
a must, a poetic cookbook
our literary collaboration—
recipes for coupled foodies.

****

I don't think I'm second
marriage material, think
that if food is love, we
can live illegally—
eat together every day.

I fantasize about
my live-in boyfriend
shopping for bamboo
kitchenware—
spoon-spatulas
and an adjustable whisk
tucked into his stocking
at Christmas.

Weasel Words

after Leonardo da Vinci's Lady with an Ermine

He tells me that I am beautiful, as he reaches for my left breast.

I tell him that I want to *talk* first, that I want to know

more about him, first, want to know more about his family,

his seven siblings, his two boys, his mother, father.

More than his online profile.   The sun has just set.

He obliges by placing his head on my lap, his gaze fixes skyward,

his legs bend at the knees. He makes himself comfortable

on that wooden bench by the lake, begins, a bit rehearsed,

as if he's on the psychiatrist's couch.   Then, he locks eyes,

mine to his, magnet-like, and without equivocation says,

God, you are beautiful.   He paws at my left breast.

I look away like a model.

This Stone

I find

a stone

shaped like a penis

hard stone

river-smoothed stone

cold to the first touch

sit it on the ledge

penis stone

bridge railing

warms in the sun

warms in the hollow

of my hand

warms hot when

I rub it

palm-sized

grey with veins

fine black and tan veins

but mostly grey

penis of stone

I find on my birthday

walk where creek

spills into river

freeway rushes

like water

wish upon

a stone

shaped like a penis

rub it

like a genie's lamp

How many hands have touched this stone? Is it a virgin stone?

How are stones born? Landslides? Mudslides? A tilt of the silt?

Educated and shaped by the wisdom of water, this stone, a penis.

This stone will outlive me.

Why do I always think of death on my birthday?

Maybe, it's the desire, to close the circle,

carve into the headstone the end date after the dash—

put punctuation to my life.

The last meal we had together—

I order shrimp salad, and you order stone soup.

Gone

Brick-heavy heart, like this Tampa street, last brunch eaten.

Truth: we hurt because we love and love because we hurt.

Emilio

He puts his boots on the table,

designer leather boots he'd bought

when he went to see his mother, his last trip

back to Italy.

  Puts his boots on the craps table

   side zip closure, python, black and white

   pointed toe, ankle boots, handmade

   leather sole.

His boots on the craps table, as if they were chips

on the pass line, his boots exchanged for an $1100

black marker; he wins big with 7, and then 11,

rolls a 2 and then a 3, loses one shoe.

  Threadbare socks, at the craps table

   dice tumbles to a 12, he loses the other,

   places a collect-call to me, tells me this story,

   what he's been up to for two days.

Needs money for shoes, a bus ticket from Vegas

and, only after he swears he's done, no more,

he's learned his lesson, promises to stop gambling,

do I Western Union the money, plus extra for food.

Another collect-call, one day later, Emilio

buys sneakers, loses the rest at roulette.

Tell me Your Lie

the one about how you want me:

    how you're going to kiss me:

        a hundred hellos.

Tell me your lie:

the one about what my body does to you:

    how driving to your dentist, thinking of me:

        makes you hard.

Tell me your lie:

the one about how you're going to take me:

    to a nice restaurant, allow me to choose:

        from the menu myself, instead of ordering:

            for me, allow me to order a salad:

                that you won't make that face, the wincing one.

Tell me your lie:

that I will be your *only one*, under the moon, under the sun:

    forever and always:

        always and forevermore.

Tell me your lie:

the one about how you've changed:

how you're not sleeping with anybody else:

how you're not drinking:

how you're not a liar anymore.

Tell me your lie: I will believe you.

The End, Again

I block him so I'd never see another post,
after all, he was the sort to over boast.

Guess I'm always the ever-pleasing host
yearning to make breakfast, biscuits or toast,

plan a romantic get-a-way to the Amalfi coast.
Seems like every lover for me turns to ghost.

The doctor says, *another broken heart diagnosed.*
Now, reading again, *How to Keep a Man Engrossed.*

Victoria Dym is a graduate of Ringling Brothers Barnum and Bailey Clown College with a degree in Humility, a Bachelor of Arts, in Philosophy, from the University of Pittsburgh, and a Masters of Fine Arts, Creative Writing-Poetry from Carlow University. Her two poetry chapbooks, *Class Clown*, and *When the Walls Cave In* were published by Finishing Line Press in 2015 and 2018.

Ms. Dym was cast for the Risk! Live from Orlando storytelling show and her story, *One Shot* was selected for the podcast. Her short story, *The Linzer Torte* was published in <u>The Scribe Magazine</u>, January 2020 issue.

Victoria is currently submitting her full-length poetry manuscript, *The Hatchet Sun*, and two new chapbooks, *Shaving the* Yak, and *There Are No Dogs on Mars, and Other Sermons from the Dog Chapel* for publication.

She lives in Tampa Florida, where she hosts the Annual October Haiku Challenge, teaches poetry, storytelling, and facilitates Laughter Yoga workshops for Cano Health Wellness Centers. Victoria is the co-founder of The Metanoia Retreat for Writers, Well-Being and Right Whales on Amelia Island. Ms. Dym performed her first solo improv show, *The Haiku Lady*, at the Countdown Improv Festival in 2021.

~

Many thanks to Poet Laureate Katherine Nelson-Born of The West Florida Literary Federation for selecting, *Spontaneous*, as the winner of the 2021 Poem-A-Day Challenge and my guide to getting this chapbook to publication. Constant genuflecting forever goes to my poetry workshop crew, M. A., Martha and Cath, for every other Monday workshopping, and sometimes emergency, editing sessions. To Barbara, who checked-in daily on my progress and mental stability in November, during the writing of thirty prompted poems in thirty days, thank you, thank you, thank you. Grateful always to my daughter, Sydney, for making me a better human, and for being proud of her clown-poet mother, as her clown-poet mother is so very proud of her.

Made in United States
Orlando, FL
23 March 2022

16081244R00028